Under His Wings

Micki Augustus

BookLeaf Publishing

India | USA | UK

Presentation by *BookLeaf Publishing*

Web: www.bookleafpub.com

E-mail: info@bookleafpub.com

ISBN: 9789363306745

First edition 2024

*To my Heavenly Father and the Lord Jesus
Christ,*

*Thank you for your loving kindness and your
gift of salvation! To you, I give glory and praise
and honor forever and ever!*

ACKNOWLEDGMENT

I want to acknowledge my husband, Bret. His love and support have been a blessing to me. Thank you!

PREFACE

I hope that you will enjoy reading these poetic poems of prayer and praise. Christ Jesus has changed my life. When I felt lost, hurt, and alone, I would cry out to Jesus in my distress, and He never failed to comfort me, save me, and give me rest. I pray that you will join me in giving Him honor and glory forevermore!

Glory to the King

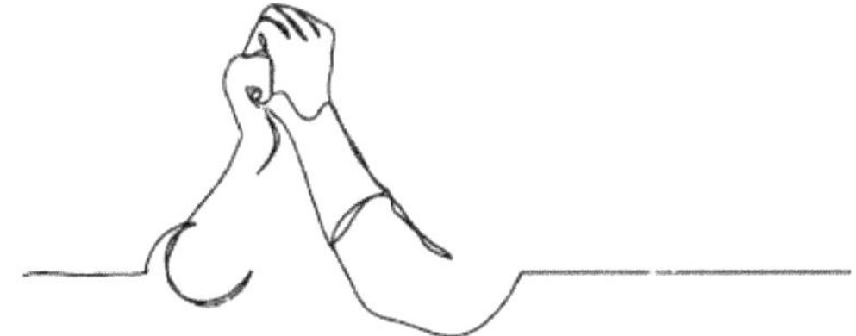

My Heavenly Father,

How great and mighty you are, my King!
When we obey, you do great and mighty things!

For we are marked and sealed with your Holy
Spirit,
Your anointing upon us, nothing can compare to
it.

Your mighty name we will proclaim,
Your love and faithfulness forever remain.

You, my Lord, appoint all things,
Songs of thanksgiving and praise we will sing.

You make the impossible possible,
you make blessings come from the mess.
You redeem the parts we thought were wasted,
you do not hesitate to bless.

Heavenly Father, you remain the same,
King above all kings, forever you will reign!

You, my LORD, are the only way,
You, my King, I will praise every day!

Thank you, Jesus, thank you my King,
Thank you for being my everything!

Jesus, I pray in your name, I pray in your power
Thank you for hearing my prayer, my heavenly
Father!

All glory to you, God!
Forever and ever and forevermore!
Amen & Amen

None So True

Lord, there is none like you
No Lord, there is none so true.

Your forgiveness purifies us white as snow
Your grace is more than we can know
Your mercy is new every day
You gave your life to make a way
Your love has no measure
Your kindness, we find pleasure
Your joy gives strength
Your goodness, you do not forsake
Your faithfulness is seen all around
Your salvation can be found

No Lord, there is none so true
Lord, there is none like you.

Grace

Lord, I want my heart to be aligned with you,
I don't want to go on feeling so blue.

Lord, You give the birds and the bees a new
song,
Fill me with your words so I can sing along.

Lord, You awaken the day with the sun so
bright,
It fills the sky with your magnificent light;
The living colors of your amazing grace,
The hope of a new day I will face.

Your majesty, my King,
A song of praise I will sing.
Great is your love, so pure, so true,
Fill me with your strength to help me through.

Lord, you love me, this I know;
For your word tells me so.
I bow my head, I pray to you,
Fill me with your spirit, make me new.

Lord, all of creation soon will see,
When you come again in great glory!
On that day filled with light,
The sky will be oh so bright!

I will wait patiently for you, my King;
For on that day when all of creation will sing.
You will gather me in your arms and hold me
tight,
There will be no more struggle, no more fight.

I will finally be with you, face to face,
All because of your amazing grace.

Woman of Valor

A woman of valor, she is a soldier.

She is both strong and delicate.
She is both strict and kindhearted.
She is both protector and defender.
She is both unbreakable and gracious.

A woman of valor, she is a soldier.

She is full of love and courage.
She is full of determination and boldness.
She is fearless and firm.
She is gentle and brave.

A woman of valor, she is a soldier.

She has heart.
She has spirit.

She loves.
She serves.

A woman of valor, she is a soldier.

She is a woman of learning.
She is a woman of kindness
She is a woman of compassion.
She is a woman of faith.

A woman of valor, she is a soldier.

She is a woman of leadership.
She is a woman of prayer.
She is a woman of peace.
She is a woman of courage.

A woman of valor, she is a soldier.

She loves, She serves,
She fears the LORD GOD Almighty!

She is a soldier. She is a woman of valor!

I Need You

Jesus, I need you
O, Lord yes I do
Jesus, I need you
I feel so blue

My heart is hurting, I feel so much pain
My life is like a never-ending rain,
I sit and wonder
With nothing do I gain,
I sit and ponder
Trying to ignore this aching pang.

Jesus, I need you
O, Lord yes I do
Jesus, I need you
I feel so blue

Many questions do I find
No answers to fill my mind
Come quickly Lord, come fast
Please make this all end, at last.

Jesus, I need you
O, Lord yes I do
Jesus, I need you
Please come and make me feel new

Jesus, I need you
O, Lord yes I do.
Jesus, I need You

Remember

I sit in the storm and see the lightning,
It flashes so bright, and it is so blinding!

I hear the roaring thunder too.
You, O Lord, have made me remember anew.

I Remember your redeeming power; I remember
your sweet grace,
I will remember as I look upon your glorious
face.

You are mine and I am yours
I sit and I remember as the thunder roars!

My Redeemer, my Rock, my Lord who is above
I will remember, my Lord, you are my first true
love!

Preparing for Battle: A Warrior's Prayer Poem

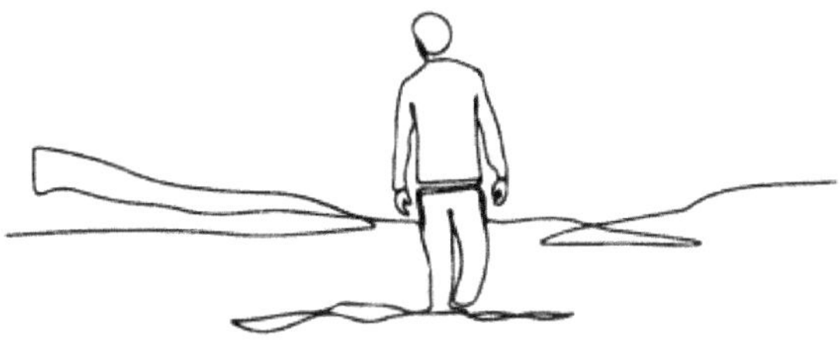

My Father who is in Heaven,

Your warrior comes to prepare for battle,
I have no horse; I have no saddle.
The enemy is stalking me,
He's around every corner and around every tree!

I pray to you, Lord, help me to stand,
I will obey your truth and your every command.
God Almighty, you have already won,
Jesus said, "it is finished, it is done!"

I will take my Bible from the shelf,
With the truth of your word, I will girdle myself.
I will buckle your truth and I will stand firm,
I will make the enemy wiggle and make him
squirm!

I will put on the breastplate of the righteous
One,
I will guard my heart from the enemy's fun.
I am protected by Christ Jesus' blood,
He has poured it over me like a flood!

When he sees the shoes of peace you have given
to me,
The enemy will strain and struggle, and he will
prepare to flee.
I will be ready to share your gospel of light,
I am prepared to go with a smile so bright!

When the enemy starts to shoot arrows of deceit,
I will overcome spiritual defeat.
By taking hold of the shield of faith,
I know it will protect me and keep me safe!

When the enemy is still scheming with plans to
fight,
And he starts to whisper lies, to give me a fright,
I put-on the helmet of salvation and focus on
you,
Because I know your word and I know it is true!

When the enemy starts to become stronger,
And he thinks I cannot overcome it any longer.
I will take the sword of the Spirit in my hands,

And I will destroy all the enemy's schemes and
all his plans!

Heavenly Father, your warrior is ready to fight!
The enemy will be blinded by your light!
By sending your one and only Son,
You alone have defeated the evil one!
Thank you for supplying your Spiritual Armor,
I give you all the praise and all the honor!
Thank you, Jesus, for saving me!
Thank you, All Mighty God, for your victory!

Amen & Amen!

A Walk into the Forest

There once was a girl who walked in the forest,
she knew not of the creatures that stopped to
notice.

She saw not the creatures that hid to observe,
how they all took notice of how she did not
disturb.

They noticed she walked in silence, so quiet so
true,
And she seemed to only notice the sky so blue.

She walked a little, then she stopped,
She looked to the sky, she looked to the
mountaintop.
she did not notice when she looked to the east,
not one creature, not one beast.

Then the creatures saw her move her lips, as
though she had something to say,
But then they noticed she was about to kneel
down to pray.

They stood and looked in awe and wondered if it
was true,
what they did see, there are so few.

For she knelt beside the old Oak tree,
She began to pray, for this they could see.

She knew their creator, yes, it is true!
She was one of them, and this was something
new!

She prayed to The One Most High,
she prayed to the King,
she prayed to The One that is unseen!

The creatures then they knew
That this is the girl that could be true.

They welcomed her into their world as they
began to appear,
showing the girl that they were near.

She arose to her feet and began to see,
The creatures surround her

The birds and the bee.

The girl noticed the flowers opened wide their
petals,
The girl noticed the beasts standing in the
meadows

She lifted her eyes to see the mighty one,
The Eagle that flew and danced in the sun.

She began to join the creatures and beasts
In a song of joy, a song of peace.

And a song came forth, of thanks and praise,
As they all rejoiced in the Lord's amazing grace!

The girl in the forest who walks amongst the
trees,
The creatures noticed she did not even disturb
the leaves.

For the creatures and the beast did see her go,
they saw her disappear behind the streams that
flow.

For they knew she would return, once again to
pray,
and the next time the creatures would join her all
along the way.

Lament of Sorrow

How long O Lord, how long will I cry out?

How long will I cry out to you in my distress?
I come to you and I confess.
How long will my thoughts bring me stress?
O Lord, I sleep but I can find no rest.

O Lord, my God, my life is in disarray,
Will these feelings ever go away?
My Lord, I kneel before you to pray,
But I no longer know what to say.

O Lord, my God, this storm I keep-on enduring,
But I continue on persevering.
O Lord, the deepening heartache is concerning,
Where is the happiness I am yearning?

Lord, I look back on all the years,
As old age closely nears.

My Lord, I cry to you with silent tears,
O Lord, I have told you of all my fears.

O Lord, my God, look upon me and answer.

Why do the sorrows and the trials keep on
growing,
But my heart keeps on not knowing?
O Lord, my tears keep on flowing,
Tears, so many tears, that you are holding.

I trust and I obey.
O Lord, I continue to pray.
As my days grow increasingly gray,
My God, I have not gone astray.

My heavenly Father, I feel lonely, I feel sad,
I feel like I am going mad.
O Lord, how long? How long until I feel glad?
O Lord, tell me, what did I do that was so bad?

O Lord, my God, if you would just give me a
word,
Clear my eyes so they are not so blurred.

O Lord, will you let my soul fly like a bird?
Fly away from what has occurred
and feels so absurd.

I would fly high into the sky,
O Lord, I would fly away without a goodbye.
Lord, there is no one to look up, no one to cry,
Lord, no one standing, their heaviness to sigh.

I would leave the wind to blow,
I would leave the mountain tops of snow,
O Lord, I would leave the earth far below,
I would soar high to heavens' glow!

O Lord, there among the angels the heartache
and sorrows would finally cease,
O Lord, there among the angels I would find joy,
I would finally have peace.

O Lord, my God, I am tired. Will you forget me
forever?

I will wait for you to descend from above
I will wait for your spirit that is like a dove
I will trust in your unfailing love.

O Lord, my God, for you are good to me,
I will continue to wait patiently.
O Lord soon I hope to see,
And I will praise the Lord, who counsels me.

A Letter

July 4th,

My Father, who is in Heaven, Holy is your
name!
I wanted to write something for you,
something to make you smile; something to give
you fame.

My words cannot seem to form everything I
would like to say,
everything I would like to tell about you, in just
the right kind of way.

I wanted to write something for you to tell you
how much you mean to me,

to thank you for how much you teach and allow
me to see.

I wanted to write something for you, to tell you
that I am so sorry for my sin,
I am sorry for the times that I have let the devil
win.

I wanted to write something for you, to tell you
that your love means so much, and thank you for
your comfort and for your loving touch.

I wanted to write something for you, to thank
you for taking away my sin.
to thank you for delivering me time and time
again.

I wanted to write something for you, to thank
you for the storms of life;
Thank you for always being with me during all
of the toil and strife.

Without you, I would wither away, I would melt
like snow.
Lord, You are faithful, this I know.

I wanted to write something for you, to thank
you for holding my hand,

to thank you for being my Rock upon which I
stand.

Thank you for being my Mighty King and
fighting for me,
I am your princess, sitting upon your knee.

I wanted to write for you, to thank you for
straightening my crown,
To thank you for giving me a smile, when I
could only frown.

I wanted to write something for you, to tell you I
love you so very much,
And I can never thank you enough.

I wanted to write something for you, but my
words seem so few,
to give you all the glory that you are due.

My Father who is in Heaven, Holy is your name,
Forever and ever and forevermore, I will speak
of your glory and give you fame!

Amen & Amen
Your Daughter that loves you

Drawing Near

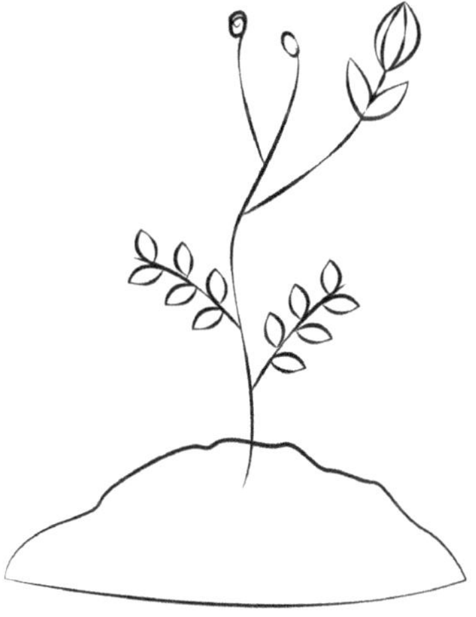

Your voice is like the thunder
Yet you whisper to my soul
Your glory is like the lightning
Yet your splendor no one can know

Your presence is my desire
To have you come so near
Yet I am so undeserving
I can only shed a tear

How can you love me so
With all my sinful ways?
You patiently pursue me
All my nights and all my days

You hold me in your arms
And protect me with your wings
You whisper your sweet comfort
You tell me of marvelous things

You wrap me in your love
So sweet, so pure, so true
All I can say, My Lord
Is thank you and I love you

The Joy of the Lord

Because I delight in you
when you follow my commands,
I give to you my peace
that you can not understand.

Because you follow my decrees
you will find,
joy and strength
that is only mine.

Rest your soul in my mighty right hand,
lift up your eyes, when you can not stand.
I am all you need when times are hard,
I am your God, your Way, your Lord

See that you never let go, abide in me,
When you do, then you soon will see,
my peace I give to you and so much more,
you are my beloved, the one I love and adore.

There Is Peace

The night comes and the thief appears
The morning breaks and there is mercy
The day unfolds and there is grace
The evening comes and there is peace.

The night comes and there is confidence
The morning breaks and there is love
The day unfolds with thanksgiving
The evening comes and there is peace.

The night comes and again the thief appears
The morning breaks with new mercies
The day unfolds with much grace and more
thanksgiving
The evening comes with your perfect peace.

Trust and Obey

Trust and obey
I am not far away
I am not going anywhere
I am here to stay

Trust and obey
When you do not know what to say
Call on me
I will teach you how to pray

Trust and obey
When you feel you cannot go on
I will lift you up

I will make you strong

Trust and obey
When life gets dreary
When the path seems dark
When you feel weary

Trust and obey
When you are afraid
When you do not understand
I am making a new way

Trust and obey
I gave you my son
He gives you life
He Loves you a TON!

Beautiful Day

I lift-up my eyes to your warming sun
I delight in the flowers you have made
I treasure your loving-kindness
Your goodness will never fade

I lift-up my eyes to see your splendor
I delight in the birds of the air
I treasure the refuge in your wings
Your comfort is always near

I lift-up my eyes to see my Savior
I delight in the Holy One
I treasure your sweet embrace
You are God's only begotten Son

You See Me

You see me.
When my day starts
When you paint the morning sky with
magnificent colors
When the dawn breaks and the dew shines
You see me.

You see me.
When my tears start to flow
When the sorrow is overwhelming
When the hurt and pain are too much to bear
You see me.

You see me.
When the sun rises high in the sky
When the oceans glisten
When the eagle soars
You see me.

You see me.
When the light within begins to show
When the turmoil starts to fade
When the pain slowly grows dim
You see me.

You see me.
With my sullen face and somber eyes
when I smile wide
when there is happiness inside
You see me.

You see me.
When the daylight fades
When the evening comes
When the moon hangs among the starlit sky.
You see me.

You See me.
And I love you!

Duel

I looked and I saw
I looked and it was no more
I looked and it appeared
I looked and it was gone.

I looked and I was amazed
I looked and I was distraught
I looked and I was filled
I looked and I was empty.

I looked and it reached
I looked and it pulled away
I looked and it found
I looked and it was lost.

I looked and I felt secure
I looked and I felt castaway
I looked and I felt wanted
I looked and I felt ignored.

I looked and it called
I looked and it hid
I looked and it was there
I looked and it disappeared.

I looked and it was Love
I looked and Love stayed
I looked and Love smiled
I looked and Love saved.

.

Everything

Lord, protect me today,
Protect me from being led astray.
Lord, guard me as I look to you and pray.

Teach me, Lord, teach me your way,
Lord, guard me from what others have to say.
Teach me, Lord, teach me through your word,
Lord, guard me from others that proclaim it is
absurd.

Lord, fill me with your spirit today,
Draw near to me as I pray.
Lord, I know you are never far away,
I need you each and every day.

Lord, when I am weary and start to fear,
Remind my heart that you are near.
Lord, hold me in your arms so tight,
Hold me with all your might.

Lord, protect me from the devil's lies,
Shield my heart from anything that binds.
Lord, I know you are the way, the truth, and the
life,
Deliver me from the doubts and the strife.

Lord, help me to lean into you,
For I know your word is true.
Lord, O Lord, I need you today,
Holy Spirit fill me in every way.

Lord, shine your light, shine your peace,
Make your enemies coil, make them cease.
Lord, send your angels concerning me,
Send them to force the enemy to flee.

You, my LORD, make all the difference,
Thank you, LORD, for your deliverance.

Lord, thank you for reigning from above,
Thank you, LORD, for your unending love.

Thank you, LORD, for your death and
resurrection
Thank you, LORD, for reconciling me to
Heaven!

You, O LORD, are my King,
You, O LORD, are my everything!

The Path

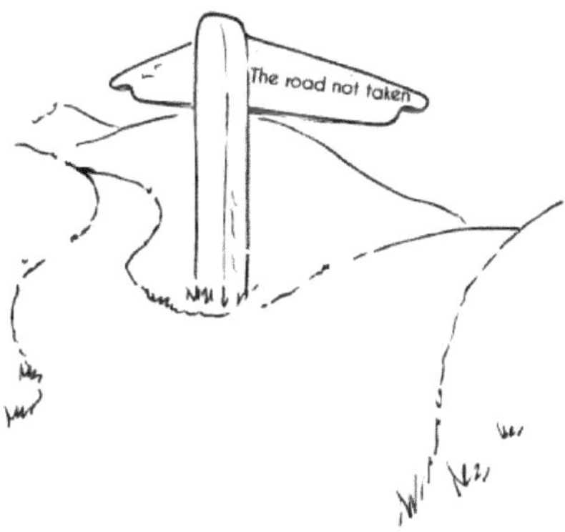

I look up to the sky to talk with you,
I can see the marvelous rich color so blue!
I see only one cloud with a soft white hue.
Lord, here I am, what do you want me to do?

Not by my understanding will I lean on,
I will acknowledge you with whatever comes
along.
I can trust in you with all my heart,
Lord, you never leave me, you never depart.

You provide a way through the forest trees,
A straight path is where it leads.
You tell me to trust you and to obey,
As your Spirit guides me, each step of the way.

The path is narrow, the one you created for me,
But your light directs my way, you help me to
see.
I sometimes stumble, I sometimes fall,
Lord, I cry out to you and you answer when I
call.

You pick me up, you make me strong,
You remind me of your love, you remind me to
whom I belong.
You place in my heart a brand-new song,
Lord, your word encourages me to continue on.

The Lord's Bounty

There is no ending to your love,
Your joy and peace, you give from above.

You are slow to wrath; you are slow to anger,
Patience and long-suffering are what you favor.

Your kindness and goodness do abound,
Your unfailing faithfulness can be found.

Thank you for giving your fruits to me,
Thank you for giving so willingly.

Salvation

He who never sinned, bore the cross,
He died for all who are lost.

He died on a tree,
He died for all to see;
He died for you. He died for me.

God, because of your great love,
Your love that you have poured out from above,
You sent your only begotten son,
Now, salvation is available for everyone!!

You're Here & You Hear

Lord, here in the present
You are always present!
You give mercies new each morning
You comfort during mourning.
You never change; you're the same as before
You go ahead; you go before.
You lead through the desert
You never forsake, never desert,
When I'm tired, weak, sore
You lift me up, like an Eagle, to soar!
My wants you know
Sometimes you tell me, "No"
You always knew
You would make all things new!
Your mercy and grace, I savor
You will always be my loving Savior!

"I love the LORD because He has heard My
voice and my supplications."
(Psalms 116:1 NKJV)

Forgive?

For all the times...

I cared,
I sacrificed,
I shared,
I comforted,
I bared,
I defended,
I gave,

I Loved...

You gossiped
You slandered
You judged
You lied
You spoke evil
You misjudged
You mocked
You wrongly accused

You hurt me.

No comfort
No mercy
No grace
No empathy
No sympathy
No care

You didn't Love.

And now, for all of these,
I…Forgive…You.

"For if you forgive men when they sin against
you, your heavenly Father will also forgive
you. But if you do not forgive men their sins,
your heavenly Father will not forgive your sins."
(Mathew 6:14-15 NIV 1984)

Then Peter came to him and asked, "Lord, how
often shall my brother sin against me,
and I forgive him? Up to seven times?" Jesus
said to him, "I do not say to you, up to
seven times, but up to seventy times seven."
(Mathew 18:21-22 NKJV)

You Are My Strength

Dear Heavenly Father,

I love how you send the wind to envelop every part of me.
The sound roaring in the trees, like the mighty ocean waves.
The trees bend in obedience to the strong current.
The leaves fall and dance in rhythmic circles.
The gentle embrace on my face as I breathe in your presence.
The crisp warmth of strength that touches my body.
The awe of beauty in your majesty
As you soar on the wings of the wind
And in you I take refuge.
I love you, Lord, for you are my strength.
Your daughter forever,
Me

"For You have been my help, And in the shadow
of Your wings I sing for joy."
(Psalms 63:7 NASB 1995)

Messiah Savior

Jesus loves you, this is true
Jesus wants to spend eternity with you

Jesus is Holy—Set apart
Jesus is the light in the dark
Jesus is God's only begotten Son
Jesus came to give salvation to everyone
Jesus died for all who are lost
Jesus never sinned but endured the cross
Jesus was crucified on a tree
Jesus redeemed you and me

Have you repented of your sinful ways?
Have you experienced His amazing grace?
Jesus is trustworthy and He is true
Jesus wants a relationship with you.

Romans 10:9, 13
"If you confess with your mouth the Lord Jesus
and believe in your heart that God raised
Him from the dead, you will be saved." (NKJV)

"For whoever calls on the name of the LORD
shall be saved." (NKJV)

The Moon Is Not Alone

In the darkness of night
The full moon shines bright
The Barn Owl takes flight
He hunts by the moonlight
Seen from afar
Twinkling Bright
Countless Stars
Dancing in the twilight
See the Big Dipper!
Look at Orion!
See the Seven Sisters?
And Leo the Lion!
Heavenly Nightlights, big and small
The Lord God made them all!

"The moon and stars to rule by night, For His mercy endures forever."
–Psalms 136:9

True Story

Here is a trustworthy chronicle that is
undeniable
It deserves full attention, for it is reliable.
Jesus Christ was sent from The Most High
He is the way, the truth, the life, that is no lie!
He came to save mankind from their sin
To break the chains of wickedness the whole
world was living in.

He was mistreated; He was falsely accused,
He endured unmeasurable amounts of abuse.
He never committed any sin
But He was beaten, tortured, and condemned.

He came to set the captive free
Sacrificed Himself, was crucified, and nailed to
a tree.
The grip of death that held the earth
He redeemed it all and gave way for rebirth.
Death could not hold Him
the curse of sin was broken
Christ Jesus has risen,
He completed God's mission!
He ascended to Heaven, He sits in glory
He will return one day, very shortly!

Take heed!
Don't be naïve!
The tomb lays bare!
Look and see, look and stare!
His body is not there!

Don't be deceived!
Don't believe the lies that have been weaved!
Upon His return, He will gather and retrieve.
He will call only those who believe!
Those who lie and deceive
They will perish, and many will grieve.

Then all will be finished,
All will be accomplished,
It will be done
by God's only begotten Son!

"On that day the Lord will become King over
the whole earth—the Lord alone, and his
name alone."
Zechariah 14:9 NKJV

REST

When the leaves on the trees have all fallen
In the coolness of the breeze of Autumn
Memories come to mind and begin to stir
Her heart breaks within her.
Laughter gone and smiles rare
As her heart lays open, naked, and bare
She looks to the mountains and longs for rest
Under the wings of His Holiness.
In the resplendent beauty of His magnificence
To be surrounded by His radiance
Tears surface and she starts to cry
She clings to hope but wonders why.

Under His wing, grace and love abound
She knows in His shadow peace can be found.
She longs to surrender the questions unending
She weeps and worships in the land of the
living.

Lifting her face to the sky
She sees the majestic Eagle fly by
Humbly, she asks the Creator of all things,
To renew her strength like the Eagle's wings.
The Father looks upon her from Heaven above,
And He pours like rain, His perfect love.
In tenderness and affection,
He adds her tears to His collection.
He draws her near
He calms her fear
He promises His best
He gives her sweet rest.

Psalm 84:1-2 NKJV
"How lovely is your dwelling place, O LORD
Almighty! My soul yearns, even faints, for
the courts of the LORD; my heart and flesh cry
out for the living God."

Promise

Here at the mountain base
You still pour out your mercy and your grace.

Morning, noon, and night,
I hold onto your promises, O so tight!
Your presence I want to taste,
I want to see you face to face.
Not a vision, nor a dream,
I want to speak to You, My King.
Above all the stormy noise
I crave so much to hear your voice.
You have already sealed my fate,
O LORD, how much longer must I wait?
Through the wind, you whisper in my ear,
"My Child, you have nothing to fear
Nothing can take my promise away
Not much longer will I delay."

"I notice every tear that you cry
Keep your eyes lifted to the sky,
I will soon be on my way
And I will hold you close on that glorious day!"

Revelation 21:4 NKJV
"And God will wipe away every tear from their
eyes; there shall be no more death, nor
sorrow, nor crying. There shall be no more pain,
for the former things have passed away."

I Will Praise You

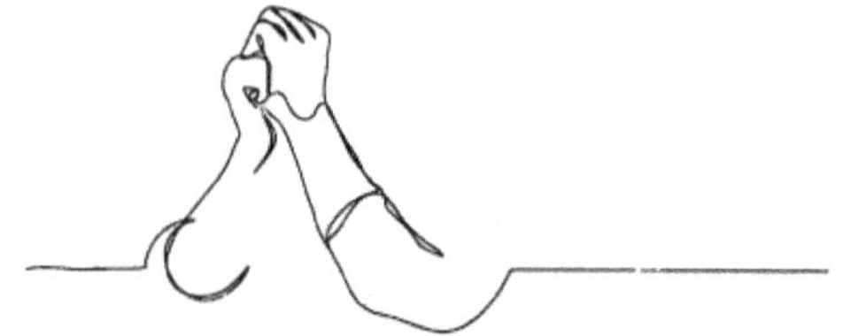

Heavenly Father,

Thank you for your new mercies today.
Thank you for not letting me stray.
Thank you for drawing near to me, as I pray.
Thank you for your love that never fades away.

I will praise you in the morning,
I will praise you in the noon day,
I will praise you in the evening,
I will praise you in the night.

Thank you for the beautiful sunrise.
Thank you for the eagle that flies.
Thank you for the cloud that cries.
Thank you for the breeze that sighs.

I will praise you in the morning,
I will praise you in the noon day,
I will praise you in the evening.
I will praise you in the night.

Thank you for the world I see
Thank you for the birds and the bee
Thank you for your unending mercy
Thank you for loving me.

I will praise you in the morning.
I will praise you in the noon day.
I will praise you in the evening.
I will praise you in the night.

I Will Praise You.

"Because Your lovingkindness is better than life,
My lips shall praise you."
Psalms 63:3 NKJV

FREEDOM

Sent by God the Father
Covered in perfect love
Transformed by Heavenly power
He spilled His precious blood.

Redeemed by Jesus Christ
Now called His friend
Rescued by His Sacrifice
No longer am I condemned.

One spirit joined with Him
Bought at a high price
Forever forgiven of my sin
Freedom never felt so nice.

John 8:32 KJV
"And ye shall know the truth, and the truth shall
make you free."

Creation

All of creation knows this is how it occurred.
You breathed out the heavens,
You sent forth your word.
You set the sun to give forth light,
You hung the moon, giving light in the night.
You gave the stars their resting place,
They twinkle across the expanse of space.
You gathered the waters and made the sea,
You planted the earth with every kind of tree.
You teamed the oceans with many fascinating
creatures,
You created the birds with heavenly features.
You made the flowers with every color and
every hue,
Every morning, they glow with heavenly dew.
With every crash of their mighty waves,
The oceans send forth glorious praise!
The trees bend and bow with the breeze,
The flowers follow along with graceful ease.
With your love, You created mankind,

Placed on the earth that You designed.
The whole earth and heavens above,
All are created with great care and love.
Created by Almighty God, for His glory.
He is the Creator, and this is the true story!

Genesis 1:1 NKJV
"In the Beginning God created the heavens and
the earth."

He Reigns

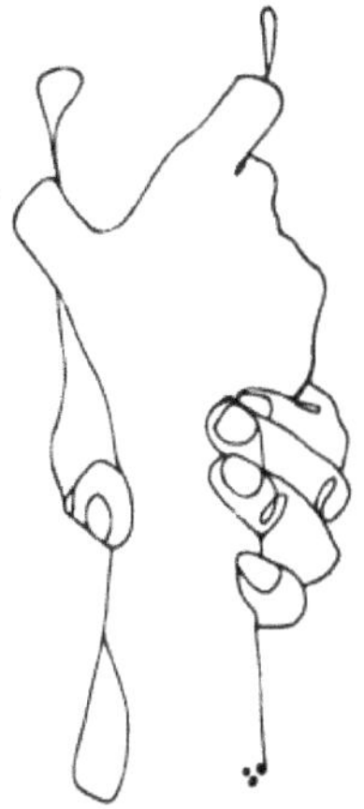

LORD, protect me today,
Protect me from being led astray.
LORD, guard me as I look to you and pray.
Teach me, LORD, teach me your way,
LORD, guard me from what others have to say.
Teach me, LORD, teach me through your word,
LORD, guard me from others that proclaim it is
absurd.

LORD, fill me with your spirit today,
Draw near to me as I pray.
LORD, I know you are never far away,
I need you each and every day.
LORD, when I am weary and start to fear,
Remind my heart that you are near.

LORD, hold me in your arms so tight,
Hold me with all your might.
LORD, protect me from the devil's lies,
Shield my heart from anything that binds.
LORD, I know you are the way, the truth, and
the life,
Deliver me from the doubts and the strife.
LORD, help me to lean into you,
For I know your word is true.
LORD, O LORD, I need you today,
Holy Spirit fill me in every way.
LORD, shine your light, shine your peace,
Make your enemies coil, make them cease.
LORD, send your angels concerning me,
Send them to force the enemy to flee.

You, my LORD, make all the difference,
Thank you, LORD, for your deliverance.
LORD, thank you for reigning from above,
Thank you, LORD, for your unending love.
Thank you, LORD, for your death and
resurrection
Thank you, LORD, for reconciling me to
Heaven!

You, O LORD, are my King,
You, O LORD, reign over everything!

Rooted

I plant with wariness
You plant in faithfulness.
I sow with sorrow
You sow in power.
I water with weeping
You water in blessing.
I grow with distress
You grow in gentleness.
I prune with keeping
You prune in teaching.
I reap with sadness
You reap in gladness.
I harvest with confession
You harvest in redemption
I root in you
You root in me.
Forevermore.

"For indeed I am for you, and I will turn to you,
and you shall be tilled and sown."
Ezekiel 36:9 NKJV

Full Moon

Starry night, moon so bright,
Nothing is hidden from your sight.
Shadows growing from the trees
Lord, I bow on my knees.
In the sparkling twilight,
Under the twinkling night,

I hear you say:
"Child do not dismay.
I am molding you like clay.
Shaped by the potters' hand,
Being prepared for a promised land."

In the dazzling moonlight,
You hold me tight.
Embraced by your gentle breeze,
My heart calms with your loving peace.

Psalms 4:8 NKJV

"I will both lie down in peace and sleep; For
You alone, O LORD, make me dwell in safety."